The Lectin Free

Cookbook

2018 Ultimate Quick and Delicious Lectin Free Recipes to Help You Reduce Inflammation, Lose Weight and Prevent Disease

By Timothy D. Murff

Disclaimer Notice: The information contained in this book is offered provided for informational purposes only and should not, by anyway, be construed as medical advice or instruction. Dear Readers; I am not a doctor after all; hence the information in this book cannot be as particular healing system. And you are advised to consult a licensed health care professional concerning all matters related to your health and your well being. Remember, you are the only one who can take responsibility for the decision you make based on this book.

Table of Content

INTRODUCTION

Let me start this book and Lectin -free journey by expressing my gratitude for you and my huge appreciation for you and for your kindness and for your precious time that you have taken to download and purchase your copy of this book.

By writing this book and offering it to you, my primer objective was to make sure that you will be able to easily understand and grasp the core concept of this book. By doing so, I only thought about you and your health and I wanted to offer you a guide that you can rely on in your everyday life. Through this book, I wanted to make, everything about the Plant Paradox and the Lectin free diet easy-to access by all of you.

The Plant Paradox Lectin Free diet has been divided into a few individual, understandable chapters, that are also divided into small parts and well-divided sections to help you focus on the different parts of the Lectin free diet.

When you start reading this book, you will clearly notice that the first chapters generally introduce to you the Plant Paradox concept while in the second part of chapters; you will find out and discover all the information you need about the Lectin free diet.

Once you have finished thoroughly exploring all the chapters of this book; you will be able to enjoy 60 healthy Lectin free recipes that will satisfy your buds and make you crave for more.

I hope, from the bottom of my heart, that you will enjoy the book and try the recipes. I also hope that you will benefit from this book as much you can.

Have a great day and be healthy!

CHAPTER 1

Welcome to the Lectin Free Diet World

What does the Plant Paradox Illustrate?

Many people spend huge amounts of money in shopping for a wide variety of ingredients and products they may or may not even use. And the wide majority of people think they are making the right choice and purchasing the healthiest ingredients. But what if the ingredients and products they are using harm their health and cause them instead some serious autoimmune diseases? And what if the foods they are eating start devastating their health instead of improving it?

In an answer to all your questions about the healthy food ingredients; comes this Plant Paradox Lectin free inspired by Dr Gundry, who first came with the Lectins concept as an upgraded concept of autoimmune diet. This book will introduce to you the unknown dangerous ingredients that may lurk into your meal plans without realizing. You will be surprised that some of the included ingredients are assumed to be amongst the healthiest foods you can use like quinoa, zucchini and even brown rice.

Many amongst you may not have heard about the Lectins free diet, but some may be familiar with the Lectin free diet. In fact, Lectins are a sort of proteins that are plant-based. Don't mistake this diet for gluten element that is found in grains and wheat because gluten is only one Lectin ingredient. Yet, to be able to completely cut out with gluten is not a very easy task to do.

In response to a mysterious trigger, our immune system reacts and starts producing certain anti micro-bodies that are supposed to fight against any type of infection that can affect us. However, instead of fighting certain infections as we expect, the immune system can attack our body. We call this phenomenon an autoimmune disease that happens when our immune system attacks, some of the healthy parts of our body by error.

Autoimmune diseases can affect different parts of our body like the pancreas, which results in diabetes, or the liver which result in ketosis. Hence, scientists and nutritionists have always searched for the best ways to improve our health and find a perpetual cure for such illnesses. And in addition to certain medicines that are meant to help our body fight the autoimmune diseases affecting it; Nutritionists have come up with some of the most important diets that can go hand in hand with the developed medications.

And on this framework, appeared the Sugar-free Diet and the Ketogenic and Gluten free diet years ago. And on the same platform, a new ingredient has appeared and is expected to have the same potential level of danger, this ingredient linked to autoimmune diseases and it is called Lectin, which is found by cardiologist and heart surgeon Dr. Steven Grundy. He came up with the Plant Paradox, and said the lectins is the one of major reasons to cause autoimmune diseases, inflammation, and weight gain.

So what are Lectins? Who came up with this new Lectin free diet? What foods that contain Lectins and that we should avoid? Should we cut out with all Lectins or should we just decrease the intake of Lectins in our meals? Are there people who can take Lectins and other who can't?

In light of the Plant Paradox and because this Lectin Free diet makes an indispensable lifestyle that all people can adopt, this diet cookbook will offer you all the information you need to know about this diet. You will be amazed at how efficient the lectin free diet will help control your autoimmune diseases in no time and how much it will help alleviate the symptoms of any chronic inflammatory condition that can affect your body.

In this Lectin Free cookbook, you will enjoy exploring the world of Lectin food lists. And you will also be able to find out what the Lectins are and you will learn the best ways to avoid it so that you can avoid any serious health condition that may threaten your life. This book offers you 60 super delicious and sumptuous Lectin Free recipes that are made by reliable, nutritionist experts.

After carefully, so much research and so much dedication; this book comes to lead your nutritious, healthy way for a healthy and wealthy lifestyle.

What is Lectin Free Diet?

Developing a healthy lifestyle needs to be accompanied by developing healthy eating habits that are not strict or restrictive; but some diets; even though restrictive, are not as healthy as you think they might be and your favourite ingredients are not as healthy as they seem to be. The concept restrictive has become confusing and healthy ingredients have become confusing too. For instance, you may think that all vegetables and fruits are healthy; yet many of the ingredients are only healthy in disguise. And because many vegetables and fruits started endangering peoples' health, Lectin free diet was developed to help you live healthy and sane. So what is the Lectin free diet?

Lectins are often referred to as a special type of proteins that are found in many types of foods like beans and grains. Many scientists and nutritionists have been searching this topic for years and the results they found were quite negative and positive. And it's only until Dr Grundy finished his result that the curtains have been revealed and the truths about Lectins came out shockingly. Dr Grundy has found that some Lectins are benign but has proven that most of the Lectins are toxic and may endanger our health and affect the quality of our life.

It may be surprising for you, but Lectins exist in more than 30% of our foods and it may be even more shocking for you to know that Lectins are mainly concentrated in legumes and grains. You may wonder what the Lectins do when it enters your body. Well Lectins may penetrate your bloodstream and may severely damage its cells by causing certain serious digestive problems and deficiencies. Besides, Lectins can also cause a severe damage to the intestine walls. And it is not an exaggeration to say that Lectins are the elements that are responsible for certain autoimmune diseases like the leaking gut and unexplained weight gain.

Now, there are different types of Lectins and different impacts on the body, but to save you all the technical data, this Plant Paradox Lectin Free diet will help keep your health under control and save your body from deterioration. Lectin Free diet will strengthen your immune system and will help your body build immunity to Lectins and other toxic elements.

Lectins are characterized by a level of stickiness that also makes them act rather as damaging elements and as anti-nutrients. And Lectins can hinder the absorption of vitamins in your body and a high intake of Lectins can let proteins enter your blood without being digested which can increase the risk of autoimmune diseases.

It's also important to note that studies on animals that were deprived from Lectins have shown an important improvement in their health condition. Thus going Lectin-free is the best diet you can adopt to get rid of all of your immune problems right away.

Eat and NOT to Eat on Lectin Free Diet

When you take the decision to adopt a new diet; then it is time to change all your dietary habits and even your entire lifestyle. And although many people are not willing to make a change they will change their mind after learning about the Lectin free Diet and after discovering its wide variety of benefits. However before starting your Lectin free diet, you should know the foods and ingredients you can eat and the foods that you should avoid and stay away from.

A. The list of foods and ingredients you should avoid

1. Avoid the use of this vegetable list

- Soy protein
- Green beans
- All varieties of lentils
- Soy Snap and Sugar peas
- All legumes
- Tofu
- Edamame
- Chickpeas
- Any type of textured vegetable
- Sprouts and all types of beans
- **Tomatoes unless it is deseeded and peeled**
- **Cucumbers unless it is deseeded and peeled**

2. Cut out with all types of Starchy Foods

- Potato chips
- Potatoes
- Bread
- Milk
- Pasta
- Rice
- Pastry
- Crackers
- Cookies
- Sugar
- Cereal
- Splenda
- Agave
- Maltodextrin
- Sweet
- Avoid diet drink

- Tortill as all types of Flours that are
- extracted from grains

3. Veggies and fruits

- Squash
- Pumpkins
- Melon
- Eggplants
- Ripe bananas
- Goji berries
- Chilli Peppers
- Bell peppers unless it is deseeded and peeled
- All fruit except in the season of fruits

4. Dairy products

- Cottage cheese
- Kefir
- Ricotta
- American Cheese
- Greek yogurt
- Casein protein powders
- Frozen yogurts

5. Savoury and meat products
- Shellfish
- Fish
- Poultry
- Lamb
- Pork
- Beef

6. Grasses, pseudo grains and sprouted grains
- Wheat Einkorn
- Oats
- Whole grains
- Wheat Kamut
- Rye
- Quinoa
- Brown rice
- Bulgur

- Barley
- White rice
- Spelt
- Kashi
- Corn products

- Popcorn
- Corn syrup
- Barley grass
- Wheatgrass

7. Seeds and nuts
- Cashews
- Chia
- Pumpkin

- Sunflower
- Peanuts

8. Oils
- Cottonseed
- Safflower
- Corn
- Peanut
- Sunflower Soy

- Grapeseed oil
- Partially hydrogenated vegetable oil or canola oil

B.   The list of foods and ingredients you can eat

- Vinegars without any added sugars
- 72% dark chocolate
- Seasonings and herbs except for chili pepper flakes
- Coconut
- Miso

- Types of flours to use
- Almond flour
- Coconut Flour
- Hazelnut Flour
- Chestnut flour
- Sesame flour
- Cassava flour
- Sweet potato flour

- Green Banana
- Sweet potato
- Grape seed
- Tiger nut
- Arrowroot
- Coconut
- Ice cream

- Coconut milk
- Miracle noodles
- Pasta
- Cappello's fettuccine
- Shirataki noodles
- Miracle rice

Dairy Products That You Can Use

- French or Italian butter
- Goast butter
- Ghee
- Goat cheese
- Grass fed butter
- Goad and sheep kefir
- Goat brie
- Plain Sheep cheese

- Coconut yogurt
- Triple cream brie
- Buffalo mozzarella
- High-fat Switzerland cheese
- Organic sour cream
- Organic heavy cream
- Organic cream cheese

Fruit

- Berries
- Avocado

Wine

- Red wine
- Champagne
- 1 oz of Aged spirits

Seafood

- 2 to 4 oz of any wild caught fish
- Any wild caught
- White fish
- Alaskan salmon
- Canned tuna
- Freshwater bass
- Alaskan halibut
- Shrimp
- Hawaiian fish
- Lobster
- Crab
- Scallops
- Oysters
- Anchovies
- Squid/ calamari
- Sardines
- Mussel
- 2 Oz of pastured-raised poultry per day
- Turkey
- Chicken
- Ostrich
- 4 Yolks of omega 3 eggs daily or 1 egg white
- Duck
- Goose
- Dove grouse
- Quail

Vegetables

- Cruciferous
- Broccoli
- Brussels sprouts
- Cauliflower
- Bok choy
- Collards
- Kale
- Green and Red cabbage
- Radicchio
- Raw sauerkraut Kimchi
- Nopales cactus
- Celery
- Onions
- Napa cabbage
- Chinese cabbage
- Leeks
- Chives
- Scallions
- Chicory
- Carrots
- Carrot greens
- Swiss chard

- Arugula
- Watercress
- Artichokes
- Beets
- Radishes
- Jerusalem artichokes
- Hearts of palm Cilantro
- Garlic
- Red and green leaf lettuce
- Kohlrabi
- Mesclun
- Parsley
- Basil
- Daikon radishes
- Okra
- Fennel
- Butter lettuce
- Escarole
- Endive
- Asparagus
- Mustard greens
- Mizuna
- Mint
- Leafy greens
- Romaine
- Spinach
- Perilla
- Purslane
- Seaweed
- Dandelion greens
- Algae
- Mushrooms
- Sea vegetables

Bread and Bagels

- Bread and bagels made with almond flour
- Siete brand tortillas made with coconut flour
- Paleo coconut flakes cereal
- Paleo Wraps
- Green Bananas
- Green plantains

Veggies

- Cassava
- Sweet potatoes or yams
- Parsnips
- Yucca
- Celery root
- Baobab fruit

- Rutabaga
- Persimmon
- Taro roots
- Glucomannan
- Tiger nuts
- Jicama

- Turnips
- Millet Sorghum
- Green Papaya
- Green mango
- Millet Sorghum

Meat

- Grass fed pork
- Beef
- Bison
- Lamb

- Prosciutto
- Wild game
- Venison Boar
- Elf

Plant based meats

- Hemp tofu
- Veggie burger
- Quorn

- Hilary's root
- Grain free Tempeh

Oils

- Algae oil
- Olive oil
- Coconut oil
- Macadamia oil
- MCT oil
- Avocado oil

- Perilla oil
- Rice bran oil
- Sesame oil
- Red palm oil
- Flavoured cod liver oil
- Walnut oil

Sweeteners

- Inulin
- Monk fruit
- Luo han guo

- Yacon
- Stevia
- Erythritol
- Xylitol

Seeds and Nuts

- Macadamia per day
- Pecans
- Walnuts
- Pine Nuts
- Pistachios
- Coconut
- Pecans
- Chestnuts

- Coconut Cream Hazelnuts
- Hemp seeds
- Sesame Seeds
- Psyllium
- Hemp protein powder
- Pine Nuts
- Brazil nuts

➢ Note

Many rely on what we know for sure: Some Lectins are toxic. But no one eats those! For example, Lectins in raw or undercooked kidney beans can cause symptoms that mimic food poisoning, such as vomiting and diarrhea. But that doesn't mean no one should eat any beans— it just means we can't eat raw kidney beans.

Tips of Adopting the Lectin Free Diet

Adopting any new diet can be frustrating and difficult at first, and starting anything new lifestyle is difficult as well. The same can be said about the Lectin free diet; although this diet is very healthy and known for the huge benefits it has for your health, but we can't cut with Lectin-rich foods all of a sudden. So, don't panic and don't be frustrated, because there are a few tips that you can follow to be able to gradually start reducing the Lectins from your food.

Now, no one can wipe out the intake of Lectins all at once; so cutting the Lectin-heavy ingredients has to take place in steps. And that you have started to live Lectin-free; you should remember the following:

1. Peel and deseed all the vegetables and the fruits

Start by peeling and deseeding all the fruits and the veggies before using or eating it. You may wonder why you should do that and the answer is simple. Most of the Lectins are usually found in the seeds and the skins of the plants.

2. What to purchase and what not to purchase?

When you shop for fruits, purchase the in-season fruits, because Next, shop for in-season fruits, which contain very few Lectins in comparison to pre-ripe fruits.

3. Always prepare the legumes with the pressure cooker

Using a pressure cooker to cook legumes is the best cooking technique that can use to destroy Lectins. So, if you have decided to go Lectin-free, you should pressure cook your legumes first.

4. Stop using brown rice and use white rice instead.

If you are using brown rice instead of white rice because you think it is healthier, you can give up on that and switch back to the use of white rice. Brown rice and whole grains in general; have proven that whole grains can cause serious digestive distresses in your stomach, so it is better to keep whole grains away.

5. Only use Grass-Fed ground beef

Doctors have discovered that the Plant paradox diet is based on using grass-fed ground beef in general. Thus, farmers have started raising grass-fed meat instead of the meat they used to raise. You can use grass-fed meat in making all burgers and all your dishes as well.

6. Use dark chocolate instead of chocolate with milk

Always make sure to use dark chocolate instead in chocolate with milk; the higher the percentage of the chocolate, the darker the chocolate is. Indeed, the darker the chocolate is, the less the sugar it contains. You can start with about 72% dark chocolate.

7. What we should do to neutralize Lectins?

Sprouting grains and beans or seeds lowers the content of Lectin in your food; so make sure to neutralize your food by sprouting it before cooking it. And the longer the period you sprout your grains, the more the Lectins become deactivated.

8. Soak some ingredients before using it

Soaking is one of the most traditional and effective Lectin reduction techniques used on earth. You can use the soaking method to cook the beans and the grains. And to do that, just soak the beans and the legumes for an overnight; then change the water very often. Rinse and drain the ingredients before cooking it; then add the sodium bicarbonate because it can help neutralize the Lectins better.

9. Fermenting

Fermentation usually allows beneficial bacteria to convert many harmful elements in your food. This process may be the healthiest method different cultures used to ferment grains.

10.   Stop purchasing bread and make your tortillas at home

In addition to representing a healthy practice, tortillas can be fun to make especially on weekends. You can make your tortillas with cassava flour and a very few ingredients. So how about starting the new family tradition of making tortillas?

➤ Note

Whether you are new to Lectin-free diet or you have started it for a while; the previous tips will help you get started with your Lectin free diet correctly

Benefits and Possible Risks of Lectin Free Diet

If you are not following a certain diet and you want to improve your health; Plant Paradox Lectin Free diet makes a great choice as can alleviate the symptoms of many food sensitivities. Besides, Lectin Free diet has many benefits:

1. Benefits of Lectin Free Diet

a. **Eating huge amount of foods that contain Lectins may endanger your life**; but following a Lectin free diet can improve your digestive system. Besides, Lectin free diet can relieve the symptoms of gastric problems.

b. **Adopting Lectin Free diet can help you avoid any toxic foods** that may threaten your health. Pressure cooking destroys most of the Lectins too. So to enjoy a healthy life; avoid eating raw or undercooked ingredients.

c. **Lectin Free diet can help reduce the peptic ulcers**

An animal study showed the negative effects of Lectin in rats. It spiked bacterial growth in the small intestine and stripped away the mucous defense layer. This increases the risk of peptic ulcers.

d. **Plant Paradox Lectin Free diet may help you avoid damage in your digestive tract**

Some researchers have found that Lectins can disrupt the process of digestion and cause serious damage to the intestines, especially if eaten in huge amounts. Adopting the Lectin Free diet can resolve this problem.

2. **Possible Risks of Lectin Free Diet**

Many of the foods that eliminate the use of Lectins are beneficial for your health; but you have to make sure to eat vegetables and fruits to compensate the intake of fiber and supplements.

3. **Lectin Free diet is promising, but there is still a lack of information on this diet**

Although many nutritionists and scientists have researched the Lectin free diet; most of the studies have been made on animals not human beings. Thus, more details should be conducted on the topic.

➢ **Note**

It is quite impossible to avoid the existence of Lectins in your foods. Yet, there are methods and ways to decrease the intake of Lectins gradually before cutting out with it once and for all. So, what are you waiting for to start your Lectin free diet and neutralize you toxic ingredients now.

Chapter 2

Breakfast Recipes

Recipe 1: Breakfast Pancakes with Cassava flour

SERVES 4

A fluffy and light cinnamon pancakes made with Lectin-free ingredients. You will enjoy this breakfast recipe made with goat milk and Cassava flour. This recipe is energetic and won't cause any digestive troubles.

INGREDIENTS

- 2 tablespoons monk's fruit sweetener
- 1 tablespoon of baking powder
- 1 teaspoon of cinnamon plus more for serving
- 1 cup cassava of flour
- 1/4 teaspoon of sea salt
- 1/8 teaspoon of nutmeg
- 1 1/4 cup of coconut/almond yogurt or goat's milk kefir to the room temperature
- 1/2 teaspoon of vanilla extract
- 2 large eggs to the room temperature
- 3 tablespoons of melted butter
- 1/4 Cup of water

Directions

1. Start by preheating a non-stick griddle to a medium-low heat.
2. Whisk the sweetener, baking powder with the flour, the cinnamon, the sea salt, and the nutmeg in a large bowl until everything is combined.
3. Whisk the vanilla and the eggs with the kefir/yogurt and the water in a bowl until everything is well combined.
4. Add the butter into the kefir mixture

PREP TIME

35 Minutes

Total Time

35 Minutes

MACROS

18% Fat

3% Carbs

16% Protein

Lectin Free

Gluten Free

Vegetarian

Pour and cook

Less than 40 minutes

5. Mix the wet mixture with the dry one in a bowl
6. Take 1/4 measuring cup so that you can use to pour the batter on the griddle
7. Cook until you see bubbles; then flip with a spatula
8. Repeat the same process with the remaining mixture
9. Sprinkle a little bit of cinnamon
10. Serve and enjoy

Recipe 2: Breakfast cream with Chocolate

SERVES 2

Lectin Free, healthy, creamy and smooth; this breakfast recipe makes a nice bowl to enjoy anytime you wake up. Besides, this recipe is very easy to make and doesn't need more than a few minutes.

INGREDIENTS

- To make the ice cream
- 1 and ½ large organic frozen bananas
- 1 cup of organic frozen cauliflower rice
- 1/4 cup and 1 tablespoon of homemade almond milk
- 2 tablespoons of organic almond butter

Toppings:

- 1/2 cup of organic wild blueberries

PREP TIME

5 Minutes

Total Time

5 Minutes

MACROS

14 % Fat

Directions

1. Add all your ingredients for the cream into a blender and blend very well on a high speed
2. Transfer your mixture to serving bowls
3. Top with the suggested toppings
4. Serve and enjoy!

1. 5 % Carbs

9 % Protein

Lectin Free

Vegan

Gluten Free

Vegetarian

Blended

Less than 10 minutes

Recipe 3: Breakfast Sweet Potato Toast

SERVES 3-4

You have recently adopted the Gluten free diet and you don't know what to eat at breakfast? You don't know what ingredients you can use to enjoy a delicious breakfast; then this recipe is the one for you.

INGREDIENTS

- 1 to 2 large sweet potatoes
- Any toppings of your choice

Directions

PREP TIME

6 Minutes

Total Time

10 Minutes

1. Start by vertically slicing the sweet potatoes into slices of ¼ inch of thickness; you can peel the potatoes or leave it with the skin on	MACROS
	15 % Fat
2. Turn your toaster on high and toast the potato for about 2 rounds for about 5 minutes	3 % Carbs
	13 % Protein
3. Spread the potato toasts with toppings of your choice	Lectin Free
4. Serve and enjoy your toast!	Vegetarian
	Gluten Free
	Paleo Friendly
	Made in the toaster
	Less than 5 minutes

Recipe 4: Aloo Gobi Breakfast

SERVES 3-4

One of the best authentic dishes, this recipe can be your next favourite Lectin free breakfast recipe. This breakfast is packed with vitamins and proteins; you will enjoy this recipe for sure.

INGREDIENTS

- 3 Finely minced garlic cloves
- 1 Tablespoon of finely minced ginger
- 2 Teaspoons of ground coriander
- 1/2 teaspoon of ground turmeric
- 1/4 teaspoon of crushed red pepper
- 1 tablespoon of water
- 2 tablespoons of ghee, coconut oil or peanut oil
- 1 teaspoon of cumin seeds
- 1 teaspoon of mustard seeds
- 2 Cups of small cauliflower florets
- ¾ Pound of Yukon Gold Potato
- 1 can of 15-ounce of tomato sauce
- ½ teaspoon of salt

Directions

1. Put the ginger, the garlic, the coriander, the Tumeric; the red pepper and ginger in a bowl and mix with water to obtain a paste
2. Heat a huge pan that has a lid over a medium high heat; then add in the oil
3. Once the oil starts shimmering, add in the mustard seeds and the cumin
4. Cook the mixture for about 1 to 2 minutes
5. Add in the spice paste and cook for about 2 minutes or until the mixture starts darkening

PREP TIME

40 Minutes

Total Time

45 Minutes

MACROS

23 % Fat

10 % Carbs

20 % Protein

Lectin Free

Vegetarian

Gluten Free

Paleo Friendly

Less than 50 minutes

6. Add in the potatoes, the cauliflower; the tomato sauce and the salt and mix very well
7. Cover the pan and lower the heat; then cook for about 40 minutes.
8. Serve and enjoy your breakfast!

Recipe 5: Lectin Free biscuits with coconut cream

SERVES 3-4

An easy to make Lectin free and Paleo friendly recipe; this breakfast biscuits will give you a great energy to start the day with. You will enjoy the incredible taste of this recipe.

INGREDIENTS

- 1 and 1/2 cups of blanched almond flour; don't use almond meal here
- 1 tsp of baking powder
- 1/2 tsp of kosher salt
- 3 tablespoons of diced cold vegan butter
- 3 tablespoons of coconut cream
- 1 Large vegan egg

Directions

1. Preheat your oven to about 350°F.
2. Line a cookie sheet with a parchment paper and set it aside
3. Combine the baking powder, the almond flour and the salt in a large bowl

PREP TIME

15 Minutes

Total Time

25 Minutes

MACROS

9 % Fat

7 % Carbs

24 % Protein

4. Add in the diced butter and cut it into the flour; make sure the butter is cut in small pieces
5. Put a space in the middle of the large bowl; the crack in the egg and the cream
6. Mix the cream and the egg lightly; then divide the dough into four portions and roll it into balls
7. Put the ball over the cookie sheet; then flatter each a little bit
8. Bake for about 20 minutes
9. Serve and enjoy the biscuits!

Vegan

Lectin Free

Gluten Free

Paleo Friendly

Less than 30 minutes

Recipe 6: Lectin Free pancakes with coconut yogurt

SERVES 2-3

What is better than the delicious taste of Lectin Free pancakes combined with blueberries and with incredibly healthy ingredients? You won't feel you need a doctor after eating this healthy version of pancakes and you will crave for more.

INGREDIENTS

- 1 Large omega-3 eggs
- The juice of 1 lemon
- The Zest of 1 lemon
- 1 Teaspoon of vanilla
- 1 Tablespoon of coconut oil
- 5 Drops of liquid sugar substitute

PREP TIME

25 Minutes

Total Time

25 Minutes

- 4 Oz of coconut yogurt
- ¼ Cup of coconut flour
- ¼ Cup of tapioca flour
- ¼ Cup of blanched almond flour
- ¼ teaspoon of sea salt
- ½ teaspoon of baking powder
- ¼ teaspoon of baking soda
- 1/3 cup of fresh or frozen wild blueberries

Directions

1. Preheat your oven to a temperature of 350° degrees F.
2. Lightly grease a baking pan with a little quantity of olive oil
3. Place your ingredients except for the blueberries in a blender at a high speed
4. Blend your ingredients very well until it becomes smooth
5. Pour the batter into pan and sprinkle evenly with blueberries.
6. Bake until the edges become golden brown for about 25 minutes
7. Serve and enjoy
8. When the time is up, remove from the oven
9. Serve and enjoy!

MACROS

16 % Fat

4 % Carbs

11.5 % Protein

Lectin Free

Gluten Free

Paleo Friendly

Baked in the oven

Less than 30 minutes

Recipe 7: omelette with scallion and spinach

Have you ever imagined that you will still be able to enjoy a delicious omelette on your Lectin Free diet? If you haven't yet; then you should try this recipe loaded with nutrients and healthy proteins.

INGREDIENTS

- 1 tbsp of divided almond butter
- 1 Minced garlic clove
- 1/4 cup of minced scallions or white onion
- 2 Cups of chopped spinach
- 1 Cup of chopped parsley
- 1/2 tsp of dried oregano
- 1/2 tsp of dried thyme
- 2 organic eggs
- 1 Pinch of salt
- 1 Pinch of Pepper, to taste
- 1 tbsp of goat cheese
- 1 cup of arugula with 1 tablespoon of oil

Directions

1. Start by preparing the spinach filling and to do that: melt ½ tbsp of butter over a high heat and stir very well
2. Add the spinach, the parsley, the oregano and the thyme; then cook the mixture until the liquid is evaporated for about 3 minutes
3. Season with 1 pinch of salt and 1 pinch of pepper
4. Put the filling in a second bowl and set it aside

PREP TIME

10 Minutes

Total Time

15 Minutes

MACROS

10.5 % Fat

6.9 % Carbs

26 % Protein

Vegan

Lectin Free

Gluten Free

Paleo Friendly

Less than 30 minutes

5. Now, make the omelette by cracking 2 organic eggs in a bowl and season it with 1 pinch of salt and 1 pinch of pepper
6. Whisk the eggs; then add the remaining butter to a pan and melt over a high heat
7. Pour in the eggs and swirl the pan; you can push the edges with a spatula; cook for 2 minutes; then flip
8. Top the organic egg omelette with the spinach filling and 1 sprinkle of cheese
9. Season with the spinach filling and sprinkle cheese
10. Serve and enjoy your omelette!

Recipe 8: Grain free granola

SERVES 3-4

Homemade crispy and crunchy Lectin free grain Granola clusters with highly healthy ingredients. This recipe is cosy; satisfying and delicious; dairy free recipe that you will greatly enjoy and benefit from.

INGREDIENTS	PREP TIME
<ul><li>½ Cup of roughly chopped almonds</li><li>½ Cup of roughly chopped walnuts</li><li>½ Cup of roughly chopped pecans</li><li>1 Cup of unsweetened coconut flakes</li></ul>	30 Minutes **Total Time** 35 Minutes

- ½ Cup of finely ground and blanched almond flour
- ½ Teaspoon of ground cinnamon
- ¼ teaspoon of salt
- ¼ Cup of pure maple syrup

Directions

1. Preheat your oven to a temperature of about 325°F.
2. Line a large baking sheet with a parchment paper or a greased foil; then set it aside for later
1. Add all your ingredients to a bowl and with a rubber spatula; then fold the mixture until it becomes very well mixed
2. Using a rubber spatula, fold until you form clusters
3. Pour the mixture over the prepared baking sheet
4. Gently nudge the granola into one layer and make sure to keep the clusters intact; make sure to leave spaces between the clusters
5. Bake the granola for about 15 minutes; then flip the granola and bake for about 5 more minutes
6. Put a baking sheet over a cooling rack; then allow it to cool for 20 minutes
7. Serve and enjoy!

MACROS

16 % Fat

3 % Carbs

18 % Protein

Vegan

Grain free

Lectin Free

Gluten Free

Low Carb

Paleo Friendly

Less than 40 minutes

Recipe 9: Breakfast Lectin free muffins

SERVES 10

If you prefer to make a vegetarian pleasant green muffin dish; then this recipe is the best choice you can go for. This breakfast has been created for people adopting a Lectin free diet; but it is suitable for all diets as well for it is loaded with benefits.

INGREDIENTS

- 1 Pound of Turkey Chorizo
- 1 bag of 10-ounce of chopped organic frozen spinach
- 5 Omega-3 eggs
- 2 Tablespoons of Perilla oil
- 2 Peeled garlic cloves
- 2 Tablespoons of Italian seasoning
- 2 tablespoons of dried minced onion
- 1⁄2 teaspoon of iodized sea salt
- 1⁄2 teaspoon of cracked black pepper

Directions:

1. Heat your oven to a temperature of about 350°F. Line a muffin tin of about 12 cups with paper liners
2. Now, thinly crumble the sausage, chorizo in a large frying pan and sauté for about 6 to 7 minutes; then set aside
3. Poke the bag of spinach into small holes; then microwave it on high for about 3 minutes
4. With a sharp knife, poke small holes in the bag of spinach, put in a microwavable bowl and place in the microwave on high for 3 minutes.

PREP TIME

30 Minutes

Total Time

35 Minutes

MACROS

19 % Fat

5 % Carbs

25.9 % Protein

Vegan

Grain free

Lectin Free

Gluten Free

Baked in oven

5. Cut the edge of the bag and remove the water by squeezing it 6. Put the spinach with the eggs, the oil, the seasoning, the onion, the salt and the pepper in a blender on a high speed and pulse for 1 minute 7. Fill the tins of the muffins to about 2/3; then bake in the oven for about 30 minutes 8. Remove from the oven; then serve and enjoy!	Paleo Friendly Less than 35 minutes

Recipe 10: Low Carb Lectin Free Hash brown

SERVES 3-4

What all people love the most about hash brown is its cheesy taste. Besides, hash brown is only made with healthy ingredients. So if you want to enjoy a perfect breakfast and you have adopted the Lectin free diet recently; all you have to do is to love most about this healthy hash brown recipe.

INGREDIENTS	
<ul><li>1 Small grated cauliflower head</li><li>1 Large organic Egg</li><li>¾ Cup of Shredded Cheddar Cheese</li><li>¼ tsp of Cayenne Pepper</li><li>¼ tsp of garlic powder</li><li>1/2 tsp of salt</li><li>1/8 tsp of black pepper</li></ul>	**PREP TIME** 25 Minutes **Total Time** 25 Minutes
Directions: 1. Grate the entire head of the cauliflower. 2. Microwave for about 3 minutes and let it cool. 3. Place the cauliflower in clean cheese cloth	MACROS 15 % Fat 3.9 % Carbs

and squeeze any excess of water

4. Place the cauliflower in a large bowl; then add the rest of the ingredients and combine it very well
5. Form about six squares of shapes hash browns over a greased baking tray.
6. Place the baking tray in the oven and bake at a temperature of about 400° F for about 15 to 20 minutes
7. Let the mixture cool for about 10 minutes and the hash browns will start to firm up.
8. Serve and enjoy your hash browns!

20 % Protein

Vegetarian

Grain free

Lectin Free

Gluten Free

Baked in oven

Less than 30 minute

Chapter 3
Appetize Re...

Recipe 11: Organic, Lectin Free eggs in avocados

SERVES 4

What is better than the taste of organic eggs baked in avocados for a delicious appetizer? Not only this recipe is Lectin free, but is as delicious as no diet recipes.

INGREDIENTS

- 4 Avocados
- 4 organic Eggs
- Sea salt
- 1 pinch of black pepper
- 1 pinch of Cayenne pepper
- Parsley

Directions

1. Preheat the oven to 200 ° C.
2. Cut the avocado in half and remove slightly more flesh from the coreless half.
3. Break the egg and put it in a cup. Pour it gently into half of avocado. Remove the excess.
4. Bake for 15 to 20 minutes.
5. Season with sea salt, chopped parsley, a touch of pepper and pepper.
6. And presto, it's ready!

PREP TIME

20 Minutes

Total Time

20 Minutes

MACROS

25 % Fat

6.9 % Carbs

14 % Protein

Grain free

Lectin Free

Gluten Free

Baked in oven

Less than 25 minutes

Recipe 12: Broccoli Quiche with smoked trout

SERVES 7

This appetizer makes a healthy choice made only with delicious and nutritious ingredients like coconut milk because and almond flour. This recipe has proven its detox as well as beneficial results over many people suffering from autoimmune issues.

INGREDIENTS

- ½ pound of smoked trout fillet (or salmon or other fish),
- 3 organic eggs
- 1 Cup of coconut cream
- 1 Bunch of broccoli,
- 1 Bunch of spinach sprout
- 2 tablespoons of ghee (or butter)
- 2 tablespoons of ginger paste
- 1 tablespoon of coconut flour
- 1 teaspoon grated Parmesan or more
- 2 Medium or small onions
- 1 Pinch of salt

Directions

- Cut the broccoli flowers and set aside.
- In a skillet, heat the ghee or butter, put the chopped onions, the ginger paste (or spice you want), mix well and add the broccoli. Pour some water and cook for a few minutes.
- Add the spinach, sprouts, and the fish. Leave for a few minutes, turning occasionally; until there is no water left.
- In a bowl, mix the eggs with the cream and the coconut flour.
- Pour everything on the fish-broccoli mixture

PREP TIME

20 Minutes

Total Time

25 Minutes

MACROS

26 % Fat

8 % Carbs

29 % Protein

Grain free

Lectin Free

Gluten Free

Baked in oven

Less than 30 minutes

- off the heat, salt.
- Put in a baking tray; then sprinkle with Parmesan, and bake at 180 ° C for about 20 minutes.
- Serve and enjoy!

Recipe 13: Miracle Lectin free Rice Soup with cabbage

SERVES 4 to 6

A beneficial rice soup loaded with healthy proteins; this recipe makes a best appetizing dish for you to enjoy if you have adopted Lectin Free diet recently.

INGREDIENTS

- 1 Cup of miracle rice
- ½ Pound of ground meat, pork
- 1 Beef kidney
- 1 bunch of Chinese cabbage
- Some black mushrooms,
- 2 Organic eggs
- 8 Cups of water
- 1 Pinch of salt and 1 pinch of pepper.

Directions

1. Marinade the kidney with the vinegar to remove the smell for about 30 minutes.
2. Cook the rice in the 8 cups of water over low

PREP TIME

30 Minutes

Total Time

35 Minutes

MACROS

25 % Fat

5 % Carbs

23 % Protein

heat for about 1 hour, the rice should be very soft. Meanwhile, make small meatballs with the ground meat that you have seasoned to your taste; put onions, soy sauce; corn flour or cassava flour

3. Chop the Chinese cabbage and wash the kidneys, then cut into small pieces. Add the meat to the rice and let it cook
4. Add the Chinese cabbage and continue to cook it.
5. Crack in the organic eggs in the rice while it is still over the heat
6. Serve hot and enjoy!

Grain free

Lectin Free

Gluten Free

Less than 40 minutes

Recipe 14: Miracle Lectin Free and grain free noodle min Sao

SERVES 3-4

What is better than a grain free noodle that can help you stay energized the entire day? This recipe is incredibly delicious; you will crave for it.

INGREDIENTS

- 1 Pack of miracle noodles
- 2 Grass fed Pork cutlets
- ½ Pound of shrimp,
- 2 Organic eggs
- ½ Cucumber; peeled
- 1 to 2 peeled carrots

PREP TIME

15 Minutes

Total Time

15 Minutes

- 1 tablespoon of cassava flour or maize
- 1 Pinch of salt.

MACROS

19 % Fat

7 % Carbs

35 % Protein

Grain free

Lectin Free

Gluten Free

Less than 20 minutes

Directions

1. Cook the miracle noodles. Meanwhile, cut the sliced cutlets; add the cassava flour and the salt and the shrimps.
2. Cut the carrots into thin sticks. Peel the cucumber and cut it in half lengthwise; then remove the seeds and mince.
3. In a saucepan, boil the carrots for about 5 minutes (they should remain crisp), drain and set aside.
4. In a skillet, fry the cutlets in a little hot avocado oil; then add the vegetables, put everything in the miracle oodles
5. Stir; then serve and enjoy hot!

Recipe 15: Fritters with cassava flour and chives

SERVES 8-9

Have you adopted Lectin Free diet and you don't know what to make as appetizers? Don't worry; these appetizing fritters will keep you energized and you will enjoy its incredible taste as well.

INGREDIENTS

- 8 Oz of cassava flour
- ½ Bunch of watercress
- 1 medium peeled and deseeded tomato
- 1 Packet of dry yeast,
- 1 bunch of chives,
- 2 tablespoons of sweet pepper
- 1 teaspoon of salt
- Water as needed
- 2 tablespoons of avocado oil

Directions

1. Mix the flour with the yeast, the salt, the curry and the pepper and set aside.
2. Peel the tomato into a small cubes and remove the seeds
3. Chop the watercress and chives; add to the flour and mix.
4. Pour the water little by little until you get a smooth paste without being too liquid. Let stand about 30 minutes.
5. Grease a baking pan with avocado oil and pour the mixture little by little with a tablespoon to make fritters.
6. Bake for 20 minutes in the oven; then let cool for 5 minutes
7. Serve and enjoy!

PREP TIME

20 Minutes

Total Time

25 Minutes

MACROS

12 % Fat

5 % Carbs

16 % Protein

Vegetarian

Vegan

Grain free

Lectin Free

Gluten Free

Paleo friendly

Less than 30 minutes

Recipe 16: Papaya Dip with Chives

SERVES 2-3

Papaya dip has always been known for its high nutritional value and using it in this recipe makes papaya incredibly beneficial for your body. Enjoy this appetizer!

	PREP TIME
INGREDIENTS	10 Minutes
	Total Time
• 1 Green papaya,	10 Minutes
• 1 Tablespoon of Lemon or vinegar	
• 1 Pinch of pepper	MACROS
• Avocado oil	8 % Fat
• 1 Pinch of salt	3 % Carbs
• 1 bunch of chives	9 % Protein

INGREDIENTS

- 1 Green papaya,
- 1 Tablespoon of Lemon or vinegar
- 1 Pinch of pepper
- Avocado oil
- 1 Pinch of salt
- 1 bunch of chives

Directions

1. Wash, peel and grate the papaya.
2. In a saucepan, boil the water, add the grated papaya and leave for about 5 minutes (it should remain crisp), drain.
3. Make a sauce with lemon (or vinegar), salt, pepper, and oil.
4. Add it to the grated papaya, add the finely chopped chives and mix well
5. Serve and enjoy!

PREP TIME

10 Minutes

Total Time

10 Minutes

MACROS

8 % Fat

3 % Carbs

9 % Protein

Vegetarian

Vegan

Grain free

Lectin Free

Gluten Free

Paleo friendly

Less than 15 minutes

Recipe 17: Mango appetizer with lemon sauce

SERVES 2-3

Adopting any healthy diets needs so much dedication and commitment; but that doesn't mean you can't enjoy nutritious dips like you used to. And this recipe is the proof; you will enjoy it for sure.

INGREDIENTS

- 1 green mango,
- 1/2 lemon or 1 lemon depending on the size of the mango
- 1 bunch of chives
- Salad oil
- Salt
- pepper

Directions

1. Wash; peel and grate the mango.
2. Make a sauce with lemon, salt, pepper and oil, add in grated mango, mix and rectify if necessary.
3. Chop the chives, add to the salad, mix well
4. Serve and enjoy!

PREP TIME

5 Minutes

Total Time

5 Minutes

MACROS

6 % Fat

4 % Carbs

7.5 % Protein

Vegetarian

Grain free

Lectin Free

Gluten Free

Paleo friendly

Less than 6 minutes

Recipe 18: Sweet Potato with vegan mayonnaise

SERVES 4-5

Do you miss the taste of the mayonnaise because you have adopted the Lectin Free diet? Don't panic, you will discover that you can make extremely delicious appetizers from healthy ingredients.

INGREDIENTS

- 5 to 6 medium yams or sweet potatoes,
- 1 lemon
- 2 tablespoons of Avocado oil
- 1 Pinch of salt
- 1 Pinch of pepper
- ½ medium onions
- ½ Cup of vegan mayonnaise

Directions:

1. Boil the potatoes with its skin.
2. Peel the potatoes and cut it into slices or just chop it
3. Slice the onions; then make a sauce with the lemon, the oil, the salt and pepper.
4. Add in the potatoes and add the mayonnaise
5. Serve and enjoy!

PREP TIME

15 Minutes

Total Time

15 Minutes

MACROS

7 % Fat

5 % Carbs

13 % Protein

Vegetarian

Grain free

Lectin Free

Gluten Free

Paleo friendly

Less than 20 minutes

Recipe 19: Sweet potato oven baked balls

SERVES 7

Are you hungry; but you don't know what to eat because you are afraid of any unwanted digestive problems? Don't worry; this recipe makes the best choice for you with its delicious ingredients that you will greatly benefit from.

INGREDIENTS

- 1 Pound of minced grass-fed meat
- 3 sweet potatoes
- 1 Medium onion
- 1 inch of grated ginger
- 1 Pinch of salt
- 1 pinch of pepper
- Chopped chives,
- 1 Cup of cassava flour
- 1 Organic egg

Directions:

1. Boil the potatoes in water with its skin for 10 minutes
2. Puree the potatoes boiled into a little bit of water.
3. Chop the onions, the ginger and sprigs of chives.
4. Mix all the ingredients in a bowl.
5. Make small dumplings, flatten them, and grease a baking tray with avocado oil
6. Arrange the dumplings over the tray and bake it in the oven for 15 minutes
7. Remove from the oven and let cool for 5 minutes
8. Serve and enjoy!

PREP TIME

15 Minutes

Total Time

20 Minutes

MACROS

16 % Fat

5 % Carbs

14 % Protein

Vegetarian

Grain free

Lectin Free

Gluten Free

Paleo friendly

Less than 15 minutes

Recipe 20: Seared Hearts of Palms with avocado oil

SERVES 3

Do you know that the Palm tree contains more than dates; it has hearts that resemble the artichoke. This recipe makes a perfect appetizer for people who have adopted a Lectin free diet.

INGREDIENTS

- 1 can of 14-oz of drained and sliced hearts of palm
- ½ tsp of cayenne pepper
- ¼ tsp of black pepper
- 1/4 tsp of salt
- 2 Tablespoons of avocado oil

Directions:

1. Heat the avocado oil in a large non-stick frying pan over a medium-high heat until the mixture becomes very hot.
2. After washing the palm hearts, pat it dry with a paper towel
3. Sprinkle the heart with the cayenne's, the salt and the pepper
4. Add the slices and top it with the remaining seasonings
5. Cook the ingredients for about 1 to 2 minutes per side
6. Remove the palm hearts from the heat and serve it immediately
7. Enjoy!

PREP TIME

10 Minutes

Total Time

10 Minutes

MACROS

10 % Fat

3 % Carbs

11 % Protein

Vegetarian

Grain free

Lectin Free

Pan seared

Gluten Free

Paleo friendly

Less than 10 minutes

Chapter 4
Lunch Recipes

Recipe 21: Grass fed Chicken in foil

SERVES 3-4

Have you ever tried cooking chicken in an aluminium foil and enjoyed its incredibly delicious taste? If you haven't done that yet, you should try this recipe; it is delicious taste is beyond imagination.

INGREDIENTS

- ½ Pound of grass fed chicken breast or turkey
- 2 tablespoons mustard
- 1 slice of cheese
- 1 medium chopped carrots
- 1 pinch of salt
- 1 pinch of pepper
- 1 pinch of onion powder
- 1 teaspoon of garlic powder
- 1 tablespoon of parsley powder
- Aluminium foil

Directions:

1. 1 place the chicken fillet on the sheet of aluminium foil, then season with salt pepper
2. Cover with the slice of cheese and spread the mustard
3. Slice pieces of carrots and place on top
4. Season with onion and garlic, powder and parsley.
5. Close the aluminium foil by the top.
6. Put everything in the oven for 15-20 minutes at 180°
7. Serve and enjoy!

PREP TIME

15-20 Minutes

Total Time

20 Minutes

MACROS

18 % Fat

8 % Carbs

23 % Protein

Grass fed Poultry

Grain free

Lectin Free

Gluten Free

Paleo friendly

Less than 25 minutes

Recipe 22: Lectin Free Royal Paella

SERVES 4

You have adopted a Lectin Free diet and you don't know what to cook for lunch? Don't worry because this recipe will relieve all your worries by offering you a royal taste that you don't want to miss.

INGREDIENTS

- A head of cauliflower
- 1 Tablespoon of avocado oil
- 3 Large prawns per person
- 1 Pork chop
- 10 rings of squid
- 1 red pepper
- 1 Teaspoon of Turmeric and saffron
- ½ white onion
- 4 slices of organic chorizo per person

Directions:

1. Cook the prawns 2 minutes in boiling water, reserve them.
2. Clean the cauliflower and cut into florets. Chop the florets in small grains, or with the knife; be careful not to chop too long, otherwise you get a puree of cauliflower
3. Fry the cauliflower over low heat in olive oil, so that it comes to a consistency very similar to rice.
4. Add the chopped onion, pork, squid, chopped pepper, spices and finally prawns when serving.
5. Serve and enjoy!

PREP TIME

15 Minutes

Total Time

15 Minutes

MACROS

20 % Fat

9 % Carbs

36 % Protein

Grain free

Lectin Free

Gluten Free

Paleo friendly

Less than 20 minutes

Recipe 23: Chicken sweet potato tray

You are hungry; but confused and not sure what ingredients to use and what not to use? Don't panic and don't think too much, this recipe is the one you are looking for with a great pack of nutrients.

INGREDIENTS

- 2 teaspoons of olive oil
- 1 Pack of 12 Oz boneless, skinless minced grass fed chicken breasts
- 1 Bunch of green onions, chopped
- 2 cloves of garlic, minced
- 1 teaspoon Provence herbs or Italian seasoning
- 1 large sweet potato, peeled and cut into cubes
- 1 cup of reduced sodium chicken broth
- 2 tablespoons tomato paste

Directions

1. In large non-stick skillet, heat oil over medium heat and cook chicken, onions, garlic and the herbs for 8 minutes or until golden brown.
2. Add the sweet potato, broth and tomato paste and bring to a boil. Cover
3. Reduce the heat and simmer gently for 15 minutes or until potato is tender.
4. Serve and enjoy!

PREP TIME

10 Minutes

Total Time

10 Minutes

MACROS

20 % Fat

9 % Carbs

36 % Protein

Grain free

Lectin Free

Gluten Free

Paleo friendly

Less than 20 minutes

Recipe 24: Chicken Marsala

SERVES 4

Chicken Marsala makes one of the best authentic and traditional lunch recipes all over the world. And even though you have adopted the Lectin free diet, you can still enjoy this recipe.

INGREDIENTS

- 1 Pound of chicken breasts
- 1 Tablespoon of almond flour or coconut flour
- 65 ml of Marsala wine
- 2 Tablespoons of unsalted almond butter
- 1 Tablespoon of grape-seed oil
- 3 garlic cloves
- 1 pinch of salt
- 1 pinch of pepper

Directions

1. Slice the breast over the thickness, to make thin cutlets. Coat in the almond flour and remove the excess.
2. Heat the almond butter and oil in a skillet over medium heat, being careful not to burn them.
3. Brown the whole garlic cloves for 1-2 minutes; add the chicken and cook for 3 minutes on each side
4. Add the Marsala, cover and cook over low heat 6-7 min.
5. Season with the garlic, salt and pepper to taste.
6. Serve and enjoy!

PREP TIME

12Minutes

Total Time

10 Minutes

MACROS

22 % Fat

7 % Carbs

29 % Protein

Grain free

Lectin Free

Gluten Free

Paleo friendly

Less than 10 minutes

Recipe 25: *Salmon in the oven with herbs and wine*

SERVES 4

Salmon have always been known for its great nutritional value and for the role it plays in healing anaemia and iron deficiency. Besides, salmon will help you feel full in a short time; you will enjoy this recipe for sure.

INGREDIENTS

- 2 small tomatoes
- 2 salmon fillets
- 1 Medium onion
- 2 Glasses of water
- Chopped parsley
- Chopped chives
- Herbs of Provence
- 1 Pinch of salt and 1 pinch of pepper

DIRECTIONS

1. Before starting this recipe for salmon in foil, anticipate cooking by preheating your oven to 420° F
2. Meanwhile, wash and cut tomatoes into thin slices. Peel the onion and cut into thin slices as well.
3. Cut a piece of aluminium large enough and put it in a baking dish. Place a salmon fillet in the centre of the aluminium foil.
4. Place several slices of onion on the salmon fillets and then slices of tomatoes on the onion in the style of a gratin. Then add the parsley, chives, herbs, the salt and the

PREP TIME

20 Minutes

Total Time

25 Minutes

MACROS

25 % Fat

10 % Carbs

37 % Protein

Grain free

Lectin Free

Gluten Free

Paleo friendly

Less than 30 minutes

pepper

5. Form the foil by raising the aluminium up without closing it. Then pour 15 cl of water inside. Close the foil well.
6. Put your salmon in foil for and cook in the oven for 20 minutes.
7. Your salmon in foil is ready; serve and enjoy it!

Recipe 26: Cod Fish Fillet with Mushrooms

SERVES 4

Cod fish is packed with healthy proteins which will help improve your health in a short time. This recipe is extremely easy-to make; delicious and nutritious; you will incredibly love this dish.

INGREDIENTS

- 30 ml of olive oil
- 160 g celery root
- 70 g of white mushrooms
- 1 clove of garlic
- 400 g cod fish fillet
- 15 ml of garlic base and parsley
- 90 g canned tomatoes (diced)
- 65 ml of white wine
- 1 pinch of salt
- 1 pinch of pepper

Directions

1. Preheat the oven to 205 ° C / 400 ° F.

PREP TIME

10 Minutes

Total Time

15 Minutes

MACROS

22 % Fat

9 % Carbs

19 % Protein

Lightly oil a broiler pan or rectangular dish, deep enough and oven proof.

2. Prepare celery root and mushrooms. Cut mushrooms into 4-5 mm slices and set aside
3. Peel the celery root and cut into slices
4. Boil for 5-7 min until it is tender but not completely cooked, and then arrange slices on broiler pan.
5. Heat the oil in a skillet over medium heat.
6. Return the garlic, minced or squeezed 1 minute, stir
7. Add the cod fillets and sauté for 2 min; then place it over the celery root slices.
8. Your salmon in foil is ready; serve and enjoy it!

Grain free

Lectin Free

Gluten Free

Paleo friendly

Broiled

Less than 30 minutes

Recipe 27: Shrimp with Lemon and Herbs

SERVES

Shrimp is one of the best versatile ingredients that you can find everywhere and that you can make delicious dishes from it. And if you are Lectin Free, don't worry as well because you will greatly enjoy this recipe too.

INGREDIENTS

- 1 Pound of raw shelled shrimp
- The juice of 1 yellow lemon
- 4 tablespoons of olive oil
- 1 Clove of garlic
- 1 Small of bunch parsley

PREP TIME

7 Minutes

Total Time

2 Hours

- 1 pinch of cayenne pepper
- 1 Pinch of salt
- Grilled pepper

Directions

1. Put the shrimp in an airtight container
2. Squeeze the garlic clove and add to the shrimp. Sprinkle with olive oil and lemon juice. Add the salted pepper with the salt and pepper.
1. Mix gently to coat the shrimp; then let marinate in the fridge at least 2 hours.
2. Cook the shrimp for about 5 minutes, stirring occasionally. When cooked, immediately remove from heat
3. Add the parsley, then add the shrimp; then adjust the seasoning and let it cool again for 1 hour.

MACROS

25.8 % Fat

7.9 % Carbs

37 % Protein

Grain free

Lectin Free

Gluten Free

Paleo friendly

Less than 10 minutes

Recipe 28: Lectin Free Organic Sausage Casserole

SERVES 3

You are a sausage lover and you don't know whether it is okay to eat it or not on a Lectin free diet? Cheer up; now you can enjoy the amazing and juicy taste of sausage anytime you want, except for a few changes. Excited to find out how; then try this recipe.

INGREDIENTS

- 4 Organic sausages
- 2 shallots
- 3 medium tomatoes
- 2 big peppers
- 1 tablespoon of curry or saffron
- 1 tablespoon sweet red pepper.
- Fresh herbs

Directions

1. Put the sausages in a casserole, add a little water and cook over low heat, with a fork prick the sausages.
2. Cut into four pieces each and leave to brown while mixing well.
3. Put shallots, finely chopped tomatoes, curry; the chilli; after 3 to 4 minutes
4. Add the peppers that are cut into strips, add water and let reduce.
5. The sausages are already salted, it is useless to add more salt
6. Serve and enjoy

PREP TIME

10 Minutes

Total Time

10 Minutes

MACROS

23 % Fat

11 % Carbs

16 % Protein

Grain free

Lectin Free

Gluten Free

Paleo friendly

Less than 10 minutes

Recipe 29: Roasted Grass Fed Beef Tongue

SERVES 6

Don't be frustrated; beef tongue can really yummy; it can be super delicious if you try it. Not only this recipe is packed with nutrients and proteins; but it is also loaded with all the components that can protect your body from autoimmune diseases.

INGREDIENTS

- 1 Beef tongue
- 3 cloves of garlic,
- 1 Pinch of salt,
- 1 Tablespoon of olive oil

Directions

1. After cleaning the beef tongue, season it with the crushed garlic cloves and the salt.
2. Heat the oil in a casserole
3. Brown the tongue on all sides.
4. Add the water and cover
5. Cook for 30 to 40 minutes
6. Serve and enjoy!

PREP TIME

10 Minutes

Total Time

35 to 40 Minutes

MACROS

26 % Fat

10 % Carbs

45 % Protein

Grain free

Lectin Free

Gluten Free

Paleo friendly

Less than 10 minutes

Recipe 30: Grilled Bison with Veggies

SERVES 3

This Lectin free Lunch can be easily prepared. Not only you, but your family will love this delicious dish too. Lemon and thyme seasoning will add a special taste to this recipe. This recipe is practical and satisfying every time you try it!

INGREDIENTS

- 4 fillets of 4 Oz grass fed bison
- 2 tbsp of melted butter
- 1 tablespoon of lemon juice
- 1 pinch of salt
- 1 package of 1 pound of frozen mixed vegetables; broccoli, cauliflower and carrots
- 2 Minced garlic cloves
- 2. Teaspoon of grated lemon zest
- 1 Tablespoon of dried thyme leaves
- ¼ tablespoon of pepper

Directions

1. Combine the seasonings in a bowl and mix them well.
2. Squeeze a tablespoon of this mixture on both sides of each bison fillet, spreading it evenly.
3. In a bowl, mix the almond butter, lemon juice, 1/4 teaspoon salt and the remaining seasonings
4. Place the fillets on a medium-heat charcoal grill.
5. Grill the uncovered meat for 2 to 3 minutes per side, turning once. Don't cook too much

PREP TIME

5 Minutes

Total Time

6 Minutes

MACROS

7 % Fat

8.9 % Carbs

42 % Protein

Grain free

Lectin Free

Gluten Free

Less than 10 minutes

Grilled

6. Meanwhile, prepare the vegetable mixture according to the directions on the package.
7. Combine the vegetables and the reserved butter mixture; mix to coat the vegetables with butter.
8. Cut the fillets in the width wise direction, into thick slices; season with salt to taste.
9. Serve and enjoy with the vegetables!

Chapter 5
Dinner Recipes

Recipe 31: Sardine Stuffed Lemon with Chives

Sardines are known for being a great source of vitamins and nutrients; it is not only a delicious recipe, but it is fresh and it is incredibly easy-to make!

INGREDIENTS

- 4 large lemons
- ½ pound of sardines
- 1 Tablespoon of olive oil
- 1 cup of almond butter
- 4 Organic eggs
- 1 tablespoon of chopped parsley
- 1 tablespoon of chopped chives
- 1 Pinch of salt
- 1 Pinch of freshly ground pepper

Directions

1. Drain the sardines and wipe them well. Boil the eggs for 9 minutes in hot water. Let them cool in cold water. Shred and mash the yolks with a fork (the whites can be used to garnish a salad).
2. Cut a long hat into lemons after washing them. Slightly cut the base to ensure a stable seat. Hollow them up with a sharp-edged spoon, recover the juice. Cut the pulp into pieces.
3. In a bowl, crush sardines; add softened butter, lemon juice and pulp, egg yolks, parsley, chives, salt and pepper. Mix well.
4. Finally, fill the lemons with the preparation. Place in the refrigerator for several hours.
5. Serve and enjoy fresh

PREP TIME

15 Minutes

Total Time

24 Minutes

MACROS

6 % Fat

2 % Carbs

11 % Protein

Grain free

Lectin Free

Gluten Free

Less than 30 minutes

Recipe 32: Shrimp Dinner with Carrots and Sesame Seeds

SERVES 3

What is better than a fine combination of two extra healthy ingredients; shrimp and carrots? This dinner recipe is very easy-to make and easy to digest as well; it won't cause any digestive troubles, so just make and enjoy it.

INGREDIENTS

- 2 Large carrots
- 1 pound of small peeled and cooked shrimps
- 2 Shallots
- 2 Teaspoons of curry powder
- The juice of 4 lemons
- 1 Pinch of salt
- 14 Pinch of pepper
- Chopped parsley
- 6 tablespoons olive oil
- 2 tablespoons golden sesame seeds

Directions

1. Peel and thinly slice the shallots. Wash the carrots; cut the ends and cut into very thin slices without peeling. Arrange them in a hollow dish.
2. Prepare the marinade: mix the olive oil, lemon juice, salt, pepper, curry powder, shallots and parsley.
3. Arrange the shrimps on the carrots. Sprinkle with the marinade.
4. Let everything marinate in the refrigerator for at least three hours.
5. Finally
6. When ready to serve, mix together and sprinkle with golden sesame seeds.

PREP TIME

20 Minutes

Total Time

3 Hours

MACROS

6.9 % Fat

1 % Carbs

9.2 % Protein

Grain free

Lectin Free

Gluten Free

Served fresh

Recipe 33: Lectin free Spaghetti squash

SERVES 3

You are hungry, but you are reluctant and you don't want to ruin your diet? Don't worry; you won't have to go to bed hungry with this recipe. Spaghetti squash is one of the most delicious and nutritious dinner recipes that you can ever find.

INGREDIENTS

- 1 Spaghetti squash of about 3 pounds
- 1/4 cup of olive oil
- 2 onions, chopped
- 1 garlic clove, finely chopped
- 1/2 cup chicken broth
- 1/4 cup green and black olives in oil, pitted and chopped
- 3/4 cup diced cheddar cheese
- 1/4 cup fresh basil, minced
- 1 pinch of salt and 1 pinch of pepper

Directions

1. Place the grill at the centre of the oven. Preheat the oven to 375 ° F. Line a baking sheet with parchment paper.
2. On a work surface, cut the squash in half lengthwise and remove the seeds. Sprinkle the salt and the pepper.
3. Place on the baking sheet, cut part down, and cook 45 minutes to 1 hour or until the squash is tender at the tip of a knife. Let cool.
4. Fluff the flesh with a fork.
5. In a bowl, mix the squash with 2

PREP TIME

2 Hours

Total Time

2 and 1/2 Hours

MACROS

4 % Fat

1.1 % Carbs

12 % Protein

Grain free

Vegetarian

Lectin Free

Paleo friendly

Vegan

tablespoons of oil. Season with salt and pepper. Then keep warm.

6. Meanwhile, in a skillet, brown the onions in the remaining oil. Salt and pepper. Add the garlic and cook for 1 minute. Add broth and olives. Cover and simmer for about 5 minutes or until tomatoes are lightly peeled. Remove from fire.

7. Add the cheese. Adjust the seasoning. Serve on a bed of spaghetti squash and sprinkle with basil.

8. Enjoy your dinner!

Gluten Free

Baked in oven

Recipe 34: *Stuffed Carrots with Cumin and Vinegar*

SERVES 5

You are craving for a delicious dinner and at the same time you want it to be healthy? This recipe is characterized is loaded with healthy nutrients, Folate, Vitamin B6 and various nutrients that will improve your health. Even if you have a poor appetite or a weak stomach, you will enjoy this recipe.

INGREDIENTS	PREP TIME
<ul><li>4 carrots</li><li>3 chopped garlic cloves</li><li>3 tablespoons lemon juice</li><li>1 bunch parsley and chopped coriander</li></ul>	20 Minutes **Total Time** 2 Hours

- Salt
- 1 teaspoon of paprika
- 1 teaspoon of cumin
- 1/4 teaspoon of hot pepper
- 2 tablespoons olive oil
- 3 drops of white vinegar

Directions

1. Cut the carrots lengthwise into chunks, keeping them tied at the end. Steam the eggplants.
2. Let them cool.
3. Combine the parsley and coriander with salt, cumin, paprika, hot pepper, lemon juice, vinegar, olive oil and garlic.
4. Finally
5. Stuff the carrots with the marinade and arrange it in a baking tray
6. Bake the carrots for about 20 minutes
7. Serve and enjoy your dinner!

MACROS

7 % Fat

2 % Carbs

14 % Protein

Grain free

Vegetarian

Lectin Free

Paleo friendly

Gluten Free

Baked in oven

Recipe 35: Ratatouille with Veggies and Mushrooms

SERVES 5

Ratatouille has always been one of the healthiest dishes that all people enjoy. And now, you can also enjoy this recipe with a slight difference, all you have to do is to peel the veggies.

INGREDIENTS

- 1 large onion, chopped
- 6 tablespoons of olive oil
- 3 garlic cloves, finely chopped
- 8 oz white chopped mushrooms
- 2 yellow peppers, seeded and cut into cubes
- 2 carrots, cut into cubes
- 28 oz diced chopped tomatoes
- 4 sprigs of fresh thyme
- 1/4 cup fresh basil, chopped
- Salt and pepper

Directions

1. Before you start, make sure to peel all the vegetables you are going to use
2. In large saucepan, brown carrots and onion in 1/4 cup oil. Add the salt and pepper. Add garlic and continue cooking 1 minute. Reserve in a bowl.
3. In the same saucepan, brown the mushrooms with the remaining oil. Reserve with the carrots.
4. In the same saucepan, brown the peppers and carrots. Add oil as needed. Put the carrots mixture back into the pan.
5. Add tomatoes and thyme. Mix well. Bring to a boil and simmer gently for 15 to 20 minutes. Remove the thyme branches and add the basil. Adjust the seasoning.
6. Serve and enjoy with grilled fish!

PREP TIME

15 Minutes

Total Time

20 Minutes

MACROS

5.8 % Fat

2 % Carbs

18 % Protein

Grain free

Vegetarian

Lectin Free

Paleo friendly

Vegan

Gluten Free

Recipe 36: Carrots with Cumin and Coriander

SERVES 2-3

What is better than carrots providing you with all the vitamins and nutrients you need? This recipe is easy-to make and loaded with healthy ingredients that will improve your health.

INGREDIENTS

- 5 cups large peeled carrots, cut into slices 1 cm thick
- 3 tablespoons of olive oil
- 1/2 teaspoon cumin seeds
- 1 pinch of cayenne pepper
- 1 teaspoon white wine vinegar
- 2 long orange peels taken from the peeler
- 2 tablespoons of fresh coriander leaves

Directions

1. Place the grill at the centre of the oven. Preheat the oven to 425 ° F.
2. Line a baking sheet with silicone mats or parchment paper.
3. On the plate, mix the carrots and 2 tablespoons of the oil. The salt and pepper. Distribute evenly.
4. Bake for 45 minutes or until carrots are tender and lightly browned. Cool completely.
5. Meanwhile, in a small skillet over medium heat, heat the caraway to dry until the aromas come off. Using a mortar and pestle or coffee grinder, grind the roasted seeds.
6. In a bowl, mix the carrots, cumin and the remaining ingredients. Adjust the seasoning
7. Serve and enjoy!

PREP TIME

45 Minutes

Total Time

20 Minutes

MACROS

6 % Fat

1.3 % Carbs

15 % Protein

Grain free

Vegetarian

Lectin Free

Paleo friendly

Vegan

Gluten Free

Recipe 37: Mussels stir fry with parsley and almond flour

SERVES 4

Mussels are characterized by its miraculous effects on our health; it is a greatly beneficial ingredient for our health. Not only this recipe is nutritious, but it is filling and sumptuous.

INGREDIENTS

- 1 onion, chopped
- 2 tablespoons of olive oil
- 8 garlic cloves, finely chopped
- 1/2 Cup water
- 2 Pounds of washed and trimmed mussels
- 1/3 cup chopped parsley
- 2 tablespoons of almond flour

Directions

1. In a large saucepan, brown the onion and sausage in the butter, crumbling it. Add the garlic and continue cooking for 1 to 2 minutes.
2. Add the water, mussels, parsley almond flour and mix well.
3. Cover and continue cooking, stirring frequently; until mussels open 4 to 5 minutes.
4. Discard the mussels. Season with the pepper.
5. Serve with the oven fries.

PREP TIME

10 Minutes

Total Time

15 Minutes

MACROS

10 % Fat

5 % Carbs

26 % Protein

Grain free

Stir fried

Lectin Free

Gluten Free

Less than 30 minutes

Recipe 38: Grilled Shrimp with Cajun and lime

SERVES 3

You feel weak and you should abide by the rules of your Lectin Free diet, don't panic, this recipe has been written for you. Not only this dish is nutritious, but it is also delicious and packed with nutritive elements.

INGREDIENTS

- ¾ Pound of raw shelled shrimp with tail
- 2 Tablespoons of olive oil
- 1/2 teaspoon of Cajun seasoning
- Fresh chives chiselled to taste
- Lime wedges to taste

Directions

1. Soak a board in water for 1 to 4 hours immersing it well.
2. In a bowl, mix shrimp, oil and spices. Book.
3. Set the barbecue to medium power.
4. Place the board on the rack and heat it for about 10 minutes or until the wood is well marked.
5. Turn the board over and spread the shrimp.
6. Close the lid and cook for 8 to 10 minutes or until cooked through. Sprinkle with chives and toss with grilled lime wedges.
7. Serve and enjoy!

PREP TIME

5 Minutes

Total Time

10 Minutes

MACROS

16 % Fat

2 % Carbs

34 % Protein

Grain free

Stir fried

Lectin Free

Gluten Free

Recipe 39: Stir fried seafood dinner

SERVES 4

This dinner recipe is a special one that you can share will all your family members and friends. Besides, the taste of shrimp is more than excellent combined with the peeled and chopped veggies, this recipe is awesome.

INGREDIENTS

- 1 large chopped onion
- 1/4 cup of olive oil
- 4 garlic cloves, finely chopped
- 10 ml (2 teaspoons) fresh ginger, finely grated
- 4 Italian peeled tomatoes, seeded and diced
- 1 can of 398 ml (14 oz) of coconut milk
- 1 1/2 tsp of Garam Masala
- 1 Chopped green pepper
- 1 teaspoon of salt
- 2 lbs of fresh, deveined and peeled shrimp
- The juice of a lime
- Fresh coriander leaves, to garnish

Directions

1. In a skillet, brown the onion in the oil.
2. Add garlic and ginger. Cook 1 minute.
3. Add the tomatoes, coconut milk, Garam Masala, pepper and salt. Simmer on low heat for 10 minutes.
4. Add the shrimp. Bring to a boil, reduce heat and simmer for 3 to 5 minutes.
5. Add lime juice and sprinkle with coriander leaves.
6. Adjust the seasoning with 1 pinch of salt and 1 pinch of pepper
7. Serve and enjoy!

PREP TIME

10 Minutes

Total Time

13 Minutes

MACROS

18 % Fat

3.1 % Carbs

42 % Protein

Grain free

Stir fried

Lectin Free

Gluten Free

Recipe 40: Lectin free salmon with chives

Salmon makes an excellent ingredient that you can use in any dish all over the world. So if you want a quick and easy to-make dinner with only healthy nutrients; try this recipe right away and enjoy it!

INGREDIENTS

- 1 pound of salmon fillet
- 2 lemons
- 4 tablespoons of olive oil
- 1 Pinch of salt and pepper
- Chilli pepper
- Chives
- Dill

Directions

1. Make salmon, slices of about 5 mm of thickness and arrange them on the plates
2. Squeeze the lemons and sprinkle the salmon with half of the juice.
3. Mix the other half with the olive oil and pour the mixture over the salmon.
4. Season with salt, pepper and sprinkle with chopped dill and chives.
5. Stir fry in a large non-stick skillet for about 5 to 6 minutes
6. Finally, garnish the dish with toppings of your choice
7. Serve and enjoy!

PREP TIME

6 Minutes

Total Time

10 minutes

MACROS

18 % Fat

5.8 % Carbs

27 % Protein

Grain free

Stir fried

Lectin Free

Gluten Free

Chapter 6

Snack and Sides Recipes

Recipe 41: Lectin Free Carrots muffins

SERVES 8

This snack recipe is one of the most delicious recipes for its high nutritional value and for the many benefits it provides the body with. Not only this recipe is easy-to make, but it is also filling.

INGREDIENTS

- ½ Cup of almond flour
- 2 small carrots, finely chopped
- 1 minced onion
- 6 organic eggs
- 1 cup of grated goat cheese
- 3 tablespoons olive oil
- Chopped Fresh Basil
- 2 bags of gluten-free yeast
- 1 pinch of salt

Directions

1. Mix the flour, salt and yeast in a large bowl.
2. Add the eggs and oil and mix well until it becomes smooth.
3. Add carrots, onion, chopped basil and cheese to the mix without mixing too much.
4. Divide the preparation into silicone mini muffin tins
5. Bake for 15 minutes.
6. Let it cool down for 5 minutes
7. Serve and enjoy your snack

PREP TIME

15 Minutes

Total Time

20 minutes

MACROS

10 % Fat

3.7 % Carbs

12 % Protein

Grain free

Oven baked

Lectin Free

Gluten Free

Less than 25 minutes

Recipe 42: Lectin Free Carrots chips

SERVES 8

This snack recipe is one of the most popular recipes all over the world; it is not only packed with vitamins, but it is also tasty. You will crave to have more of this snack and surprisingly, it is filling.

INGREDIENTS

- 1 Organic egg
- 5 tablespoons almond flour
- 3 tablespoons of coconut flour
- 1 glass of water
- 1 pinch of bicarbonate
- 1 Pinch of salt
- 1 Pinch of ground black pepper
- 1 Teaspoon of curry
- 1 or 2 carrots according to size

Directions

1. Make donut dough by mixing the flours, a good pinch of baking soda and the organic egg.
2. Mix this dough with 1 glass of water. Season with salt, pepper and curry
3. Wash the carrots and slice thinly; make sure to peel it.
4. Dip each slice in the donut dough
5. But for cooking, cook them in a pan instead of a frying pan
6. With about 2 Tablespoons of avocado oil and 1 spoon of olive oil.
7. Put a dozen donuts, cook them for about 2 minutes.
8. Then return them to cook on the other side 2 minutes
9. Serve and enjoy

PREP TIME

10 Minutes

Total Time

10 minutes

MACROS

16 % Fat

10 % Carbs

5 % Protein

Grain free

Pan fried

Lectin Free

Gluten Free

Less than 15 minutes

Recipe 43: Pumpkin oven baked fries

Pumpkin fries have always been a quick, easy-to make snack recipe that doesn't need more than a couple of ingredients. Baking pumpkin fries in the oven makes it healthy and crispy that you will eat without realizing.

INGREDIENTS

- 1 Pumpkin
- 4 tablespoons avocado oil
- 1 Teaspoon of powdered cumin
- 1 Pinch of salt

Directions

- Preheat the oven to a temperature of 360 ° F.
- Peel the pumpkin, empty the heart with the seeds; then cut the flesh into fries (sticks).
- In a baking tray; mix the oil with cumin and salt.
- Brush your fries with this sauce (soak the fries in the tray and turn them over so they are well coated)
- Bake in the oven for about 12 minutes
- Serve and enjoy your fries!

PREP TIME

15 Minutes

Total Time

20 minutes

MACROS

8 % Fat

2 % Carbs

5 % Protein

Grain free

Oven baked

Lectin Free

Gluten Free

Less than 15 minutes

Recipe 44: Avocado cups with salmon

SERVES 3

This avocado dip is refreshing, nutritious and delicious; you can have it as a snack and even as a dessert. This recipe will improve your digestive system and you it will help you feel full too.

INGREDIENTS

- 1 Avocado
- 1 Cup of goat cheese with garlic and herbs
- 4 slices of marinated salmon
- 2 slices of smoked salmon
- 2 tbsp of thick light organic cream cheese
- 2 tbsp of lemon juice
- Chopped Parsley or chives
- 1 Pinch of salt
- 1 Pinch of pepper

Directions

- Peel the avocado, remove the kernel and mix the flesh with 1 tbsp, the lemon juice, salt and pepper.
- Divide three quarters in serving glass cups.
- Add the diced marinated salmon and cover with the avocado mousse.
- Mix the cream cheese with the cream and cover the marinated salmon.
- Cover with remaining avocado mousse.
- Cut the smoked salmon into strips and put it on the mousse, then garnish with the herbs!

PREP TIME

5 Minutes

Total Time

5 minutes

MACROS

4 % Fat

1 % Carbs

4 % Protein

Served fresh and cold

Lectin Free

Gluten Free

Less than 5 minutes

Recipe 45: Beetroots dip

Some people call it the miracle vegetable, beet is considered as one of the most colourful ingredients that can encourage you to eat. Besides, beetroot is an indispensable ingredient to improve your health and blood.

INGREDIENTS

- ½ Pound of cooked beetroot
- 1 Cup of goat fresh cheese
- 1 cup of Greek yoghurt
- ¼ cup of walnuts
- 1 lemon
- 1 tablespoon of olive oil
- ½ Teaspoon of powdered garlic
- ½ teaspoon of cumin
- Chopped parsley
- 1 Pinch of salt
- 1 Pinch of pepper

Directions

- Peel the beets and dice them. Sprinkle with oil, caraway, salt and pepper, mix well.
- In a bowl, mix the cheese, yoghurt, garlic, salt, pepper and 1 spoon of oil.
- Mix and divide in serving cups.
- Cover with beet diced
- Sprinkle with cheese, walnuts and parsley.
- Serve cold and enjoy!

PREP TIME

10 Minutes

Total Time

10 minutes

MACROS

4 % Fat

1 % Carbs

4 % Protein

Grain free

Served fresh and cold

Lectin Free

Gluten Free

Less than 10 minutes

Recipe 46: Avocado dip with coconut yogurt and fish eggs

SERVES 2-3

Many of us don't want to have dinner, so we keep looking for nutritious side dishes that won't make us bloat and that won't affect our digestive system. This side dish is really amazing and beyond imagination.

INGREDIENTS

- 2 mature avocados
- 1 Cup of coconut yogurt
- 1 pot of fish eggs (preferably salmon)
- 1 tablespoon of lemon juice
- 1 tablespoon of olive oil
- 1 teaspoon of dill
- 1 Pinch of salt
- 1 Pinch of pepper

Directions

- Peel and remove the stone of the avocado.
- Cut the avocado into pieces.
- Spread the avocado meat, the coconut yogurt, lemon juice, olive oil, dill, salt and pepper in the blender. You have to get a smooth mash.
- Pour the mashed potatoes in glasses and cover with fish eggs.
- Serve fresh.

PREP TIME

5 Minutes

Total Time

5 minutes

MACROS

6 % Fat

2.6 % Carbs

8 % Protein

Vegetarian

Grain free

Lectin Free

Gluten Free

Less than 10 minutes

Recipe 47: Veggie Chips

Are you hungry and want to eat something crispy and crunchy? This recipe will be your best choice, all you have to do is to peel a few vegetables and you will see how delicious your snack will be.

INGREDIENTS

- 1 parsnip
- 1 beetroot
- 1 carrot
- 1 tablespoon of olive oil
- 1 Pinch of oregano
- 1 Pinch of salt
- 1 Pinch of pepper

Directions

- Preheat the oven to about 180 ° C (360° F)
- Peel the vegetables and cut them into very thin slices
- Spread the veggies on the baking sheet covered with baking paper. Oil the crisps with a brush, and sprinkle the oregano.
- Bake for 15 minutes.
- Take out the chips, let them cool
- Season with salt It's ready
- Serve and enjoy!

PREP TIME

15 Minutes

Total Time

20 minutes

MACROS

3 % Fat

1 % Carbs

4 % Protein

Vegetarian

Grain free

Oven baked

Lectin Free

Gluten Free

Less than 20 minutes

Recipe 48: Peeled, stuffed tomatoes

SERVES 4

What is better than fresh and cold stuffed tomatoes that you can enjoy after your daily exercise? This recipe is delicious and refreshing; besides, it is very healthy.

INGREDIENTS

- 5 to 6 peeled tomatoes
- 1 Cup of goat cheese
- 1 small cup of green tapenade

Directions

- Wash and peel tomatoes. Cut the hats and empty the inside of the tomatoes. Remove the seeds and put the rest excess of tomatoes in a bowl.
- Add the cheese and tapenade to this bowl, and mix well.
- Fill the tomatoes with the mixture
- Arrange the tomatoes on a baking tray
- Cool in the refrigerator for 15 minutes
- Serve and enjoy!

PREP TIME

5 Minutes

Total Time

15 minutes

MACROS

3 % Fat

1 % Carbs

4 % Protein

Grain free

Lectin Free

Gluten Free

Less than 15 minutes

Recipe 49: Cucumber with guacamole

SERVES 6-7

Looking for an appetizing dish that will energize you and make you healthier and happier? Cheer up; this recipe will amaze you with its fresh and incredible taste.

INGREDIENTS

- 1 Cucumber, peeled
- 1 Ripe avocado
- 12 Cooked and shelled shrimp
- 2 to 3 tbsp of olive oil
- The juice of 1 lemon
- 2 sprigs of fresh chives
- 1 Pinch of salt and 1 pinch of pepper

Directions

1. Cut in half and pit the avocado. Take the flesh and mix it with the olive oil and the lemon juice until you get a very smooth and thick guacamole. Season with Salt and pepper the guacamole according to your tastes, then reserve in the fridge until use.
2. Wash, pat dry; peel; then cut the medium sliced cucumber.
3. Rinse with cold water; then pat dry the cooked and shelled shrimps.
4. Take the guacamole out of the fridge. Cover each slice of cucumber with a nice spoonful of guacamole and place over cooked and peeled shrimp.
5. Wash, dry and chop the sprigs of chives, then sprinkle them over the bites.
6. Place these cucumber bites in the fridge until ready to serve.
7. Enjoy your side; cold!
   - ➢ Tip: You can replace shrimp cooked and shelled with smoked salmon

PREP TIME

15 Minutes

Total Time

15 minutes

MACROS

5 % Fat

3 % Carbs

12 % Protein

Grain free

Lectin Free

Gluten Free

Less than 10 minutes

Recipe 50: Roasted Almonds

SERVES 3

No matter what diet you are following, roasted almonds remains one of the best nuts you can have. Almond plays a great role in improving your health on different levels including the health of your heart.

INGREDIENTS

- 2 Cups of whole almonds
- 3 Tablespoon of extra virgin olive oil
- 1 Tablespoon of powdered paprika
- 1 pinch of salt

Directions

- Preheat the oven to a temperature of about 360 ° F.
- Spread the almonds on a baking sheet, sprinkle with oil, sprinkle with paprika and salt. Mix to coat well.
- Bake for 10 to 15 minutes, until the almonds are broiled.
- Let cool and serve your snack!

PREP TIME

5 Minutes

Total Time

10 minutes

MACROS

2 % Fat

4 % Carbs

12 % Protein

Vegetarian

Vegan

Grain free

Lectin Free

Gluten Free

Less than 15 minutes

Chapter 7
Salad and Dessert

Recipe 51: Apple and salmon salad

Are you full and you are looking for something to digest your dinner or lunch with? If so, there is nothing better than an apple salad enriched with salmon and healthy proteins.

INGREDIENTS

- 1 Pound of fresh salmon fillet
- 2 granny smith apples
- 2 red onions
- 3 limes
- 2 tbsp. tablespoon of olive oil
- 1 Pinch of salt

Directions

1. Dice the fresh fish in small cubes or thin slices. Put them in a dish. Sprinkle with olive oil. Add the salt.
2. Peel the onions and cut them into thin slices. Add them to the dish.
3. Clean the apples; remove the stumps; then peel the apples and cut them into medium dices. Add them to the dish.
4. Squeeze the limes and sprinkle the dish with. Make sure the apple pieces are well watered so they do not oxidize before tasting.
5. Marinate in a cool place for 2 hours.
6. Serve and enjoy!

PREP TIME

5 Minutes

Total Time

5 minutes

MACROS

6 % Fat

3 % Carbs

11 % Protein

Grain free

Lectin Free

Gluten Free

Less than 10 minutes

Recipe 52: Mackerel salad with avocados and onion

SERVES 3

Mackerel makes one of the best and most versatile fish types that you can use in different dishes from lunch to dinner and even salads. Mackerel salad makes a complete dish itself as it provides the body with the vitamins and nutrients it needs to stay healthy.

INGREDIENTS

- 6 mackerel fillets
- 2 organic lemons
- 2 small white onions
- 2 avocados
- 4 tablespoons of olive oil
- 1 bunch of coriander
- 1 Pinch of salt
- 1 Pinch of pepper

Directions

1. Start by dicing the raw fish into cubes.
2. Squeeze the lemons after grating the zest. Put them in a bowl.
3. Peel and chop the onions. Add them to the salad bowl.
4. Clean and finely chop the coriander. Add it to the bowl.
5. Add the olive oil, salt and pepper, and mix.
6. Add the pieces of raw fish to the bowl and stir. Marinate for 30 minutes.
7. Peel and stone the avocados, and cut into cubes. Add them to the bowl, mix and serve immediately.
8. Enjoy your salad!

PREP TIME

10 Minutes

Total Time

5 minutes

MACROS

9 % Fat

5 % Carbs

15 % Protein

Grain free

Lectin Free

Gluten Free

Less than 10 minutes

Recipe 53: Spinach, cranberries and walnut salad

SERVES 4-5

What is better than mixing all healthy ingredients all together with spinach? This salad recipe is a nice quick recipe that you can make on the go. Spinach is rich in vitamins and nutrients that you will enjoy very much.

INGREDIENTS

- 1 Pound of spinach
- 1 red apple
- 1 cup of walnuts
- 1 handful of dried cranberries
- 50 g of goat cheese
- 3 tablespoons of hazelnut oil
- 1 tablespoon of lemon juice
- 1 Pinch of salt and 1 pinch of pepper

Directions

1. Wash and squeeze the spinach
2. Wash the apple, seed it; peel it and cut into strips. Cut the cheese in small dices.
3. In a salad bowl, mix the oil with the lemon juice.
4. Add the spinach, the apple dices, the cheese, the walnut kernels, the cranberries and mix everything very well.
5. Season with 1 pinch of salt and 1 pinch of pepper if necessary
6. Serve and enjoy!

PREP TIME

4 Minutes

Total Time

4 minutes

MACROS

6 % Fat

3 % Carbs

7.8 % Protein

Grain free

Vegetarian

Vegan

Lectin Free

Gluten Free

Less than 5 minutes

Recipe 54: Avocado guacamole with coconut yogurt

SERVES 3

Guacamole and who doesn't love this easy-to make dish that will help digest very well. This recipe doesn't take more than a few minutes to get ready and enjoy it.

INGREDIENTS

- 2 avocados
- 1 coconut yogurt brewed at 0%
- 1 lime
- 1 small pinch of Cayenne pepper
- 1 Pinch of salt
- 1 Pinch of pepper

Directions

1. Peel and stone the avocados.
2. Squeeze the lemon.
3. Mix avocado flesh with yogurt, lemon juice, chilli pepper, salt and pepper.
4. Pour into a nice bowl and serve fresh
5. Enjoy your guacamole!

PREP TIME

5 Minutes

Total Time

8 minutes

MACROS

5 % Fat

2 % Carbs

8 % Protein

Grain free

Lectin Free

Gluten Free

Less than 10 minutes

Recipe 55: Cabbage salad with Pineapples

When was the last time you used pineapple? You may not remember, but this recipe will bring to you the exotic and delicious taste of pineapples to your dish. You will incredibly enjoy this recipe.

INGREDIENTS

- 4 Cups of sliced cabbage with mandolin
- 2 cups of peeled and diced pineapple; heart removed and minced with mandolin
- 2 tablespoons of vinegar
- 1 teaspoon of erythritol

Directions

- In a bowl, mix all the ingredients.
- Season with 1 pinch of salt and 1 pinch of pepper.
- Serve and enjoy!

PREP TIME

5 Minutes

Total Time

8 minutes

MACROS

3.5 % Fat

1 % Carbs

3 % Protein

Grain free

Lectin Free

Gluten Free

Vegetarian

Less than 10 minutes

Recipe 56: Lettuce and fennel salad

SERVES 2-3

Enjoy the taste of veggies and fruits together in this healthy recipe that you will love. Get ready to nourish your body with the nutrients it needs with this fresh salad.

INGREDIENTS

- 2 Cups green lettuce
- 2 cups of green grapes cut in half
- ½ fennel, finely chopped
- 2 tablespoons chopped fennel
- 2 tablespoons chopped fresh coriander
- 3 tablespoons of olive oil
- 2 tablespoons lemon juice
- 1 Pinch of salt and 1 pinch of pepper

Directions

1. In a bowl, mix all the ingredients.
2. Add the warmed fish mixture.
3. Mix gently.
4. Adjust seasoning.
5. Serve and enjoy!

PREP TIME

4 Minutes

Total Time

4 minutes

MACROS

2 % Fat

1.5 % Carbs

3 % Protein

Grain free

Lectin Free

Gluten Free

Vegan

Vegetarian

Less than 10 minutes

Recipe 57: Raspberry dome

SERVES 5

Did you know that you don't need sugar and unhealthy ingredients to make your favourite dessert? Yes, this dessert will prove to you that you can make delicious desserts from very simple and easy-to find ingredients.

INGREDIENTS

- 2 Cups of raspberries
- 1 and ½ cups of blueberries
- ½ Cup of coconut milk
- 3 Tablespoons of stevia
- 1 Tablespoon of agar agar

Directions

- Mix the berries and remove the raspberry seeds. You can also use a mixture of frozen red fruits instead of fresh.
- Add the coconut milk gradually by measuring it; you can adjust the amount of milk if needed.
- Bring the milk to a boil in a saucepan. Add the stevia and agar agar and mix well.
- Divide the mixture into silicone glass bowls or cups and let cool, then place 2 hours in the refrigerator.
- Unmold your dessert and serve it with fresh fruits.
- Enjoy your dessert!

PREP TIME

5 Minutes

Total Time

15 minutes

MACROS

7 % Fat

6 % Carbs

10 % Protein

Grain free

Lectin Free

Gluten Free

Less than 20 minutes

Recipe 58: Flan with coconut milk and dark chocolate

SERVES 4

This dessert recipe is a sumptuous dish that you can eat without worrying that it can harm your health. This recipe is just amazing.

INGREDIENTS

- 1 and ½ Cups of dark chocolate with 70% cocoa
- ½ Cup of coconut milk
- 1 Tablespoon of agar-agar

Directions

1. Pour the milk into a saucepan, add the agar-agar and mix well. Carry on stirring on the heat
2. Add the chocolate chopped into dices and heat it while stirring constantly.
3. When the chocolate is melted, let it boil for a few seconds then remove from the heat.
4. Divide into ramekins or silicone moulds and let cool, before placing 2 hours in the refrigerator.
5. Serve chilled with fresh fruits of your choice!

PREP TIME

10 Minutes

Total Time

15 minutes

MACROS

10 % Fat

2 % Carbs

13 % Protein

Grain free

Lectin Free

Gluten Free

Less than 20 minutes

Recipe 59: Coconut ice-cream with matcha

SERVES 5-6

What is more refreshing than the incredible taste of ice cream with matcha and vanilla? This recipe is delicious beyond imagination; you will love it.

INGREDIENTS

- 1 Cup of coconut milk
- 3 tablespoons of stevia
- 2 tbsp matcha tea
- 1 teaspoon of powdered vanilla

Directions

1. Whip all the ingredients in a bowl and divide into ice cream pans.
2. Place the ice cream for about 1 hour in the freezer before poking the sticks in the ice-cream, then let it take another 3 hours
3. Serve and enjoy!

PREP TIME

5 Minutes

Total Time

4 Hours

MACROS

12 % Fat

4 % Carbs

14 % Protein

Grain free

Lectin Free

Gluten Free

Recipe 60: Dark Carrots chocolate mousse

SERVES 3

Have you adopted the Lectin Free diet lately and you miss the taste of chocolate mousse and many of your favourite desserts? This recipe offers you a healthy version of chocolate mousse that will melt in your mouth all with healthy ingredients.

INGREDIENTS

- 1 carrots
- 3 Oz of dark chocolate 70%
- 6 tablespoons almond milk

Directions

1. Peel the carrots, remove the ends and cut into cubes. Place them in the steam basket and put water in the pan. Start 7 minutes fast steaming
2. Meanwhile, heat the milk in the microwave and chop the chocolate into dices.
3. Mix the cooked carrots with the milk, add the chocolate and mix until it is well melted.
4. Spread in cups, then leave to cool before reserving it in the refrigerator
5. Serve and enjoy your chocolate mousse!

PREP TIME

7 Minutes

Total Time

15 Minutes

MACROS

10.9 % Fat

3 % Carbs

12 % Protein

Grain free

Lectin Free

Gluten Free

Less than 10 minutes

CHAPTER 8: CONCLUSION

The Lectin Free diet described throughout the pages of this book adopts the latest diet methods inspired by Dr Grundy and based on a competent nutrition research done by some of the best dieticians, nutritionists, and food psychologists ranked amongst the best in their fields. After reading this book, you will learn how to adopt a Lectin Free diet, choose the best foods for your body and eliminate all the unnecessary diets you ever tried before.

This book contains demonstrated recipes which show how the diet works. This Lectin free diet book contains recipes that will help you control your appetite, renew your physical energy, help your body muscles thrive and help you live a more healthier life in general. The Lectin Free diet has made considerable progress from being overlooked as an effective diet for losing weight or helping the body burn more fat and improves health in general. This new diet has now been reinforced by many health experts and workout regulars due to its enormous benefits to the human body, such as enhancing one's energy and improving one's overall health.

This boils down to the fact that the Lectin free diet helps your body absorb the nutrients it needs more efficiently. Getting all the protein, low-carbohydrates, and other nutrients that your body requires for optimal functioning results in healthy eating and eating management, increased metabolism rates, and more energy, all of which Lectin Free diet is able to deliver. This book provides proper guidance via strategic and exclusive Lectin Free recipes which makes improving your health very simple. This book was created to point you in the correct direction with a no-arbitrary approach to only eat healthy food.

Thanks to the proper guidance from a group of experts that the writer collaborated with, your health will improve and you will stay fit for life. Good luck! Get started with your Lectin Free Diet, we know you can do it! It's time to shed off those unhealthy ingredients.

Thank you for Reading This Book

We are very happy that we have tackled this newly introduced diet to the world and to you dear readers. We take so much pride in offering you this Lectin Free diet and we hope from the bottom of our hear that it can help improve your health. We hope that you enjoy the recipes and we are looking forward to know how this diet improved your health. Please, feel free to share this book with your family and friends to encourage them to follow the same healthy journey like you. Our dear readers, we deeply care about your health and we have sought that Lectin free diet is an advanced diet that will help you live a happy and healthy life. We are looking forwards to any valuable suggestions from your part. And we will be eagerly waiting for your suggestions.

Made in the USA
San Bernardino, CA
26 November 2018